READ ALL THE BOOKS!
HOW MANY HAVE YOU READ?

BOOK ❶

BOOK ❷

BOOK ❸

BOOK ❹

BOOK ❺

BOOK ❻

BOOK ❼

BOOK ❽

BOOK ❾

BOOK ❿

W9-BUU-564

Available at libraries and bookstores everywhere.

iVY+BEAN+ME

A FILL-IN-THE-BLANK BOOK

written by annie barrows + illustrated by sophie blackall

chronicle books · san francisco

Hi Out There!

Our teacher, Ms. Aruba-Tate, is really nice, but she has some wacko ideas. One of her ideas was that we should write in a journal every day. Every day! We were supposed to write a whole page! Who has a whole page of things happen to them every day? No one! For a long time, we just wrote really big. But then we got a better idea: we decided to make up questions and answer them, which is a lot easier and more interesting, too. We thought up some great questions! (Which do you like better, spit or earwax?)

And then we thought up some
   great answers! We also wrote
   down some extra ideas for not
   being bored.
      We decided that other
   kids might like to answer our
   questions, so we put them in this
   book. We included a few of our
   answers, but not all of them. We
   wanted to leave you guys plenty
   of room for your own answers and
   drawings and ideas.

   Have fun!

(earwax)   (spit)

My name is

Giulianna Simone tan Jarvis

I wish my name were

morgean, or Eloesy

My birthday is

(Circle the month and the day.)

Jan	July	1	2	3	4	5	6
Feb	Aug	7	8	9	10	11	12
Mar	Sept	13	14	15	16	17	18
Apr	(Oct)	19	20	21	22	23	24
May	Nov	(25)	26	27	28	29	
June	Dec	30	31				

Year 2010

My family has <u>losts</u> of **people in it.**
They are

Vary nice thay take care
of me and love me. thar
like rianeBow's and Flowers and
Sunsine all tgethere
(and gems)

My sister
Nancy looks
like this!

They look like this

My friend's name is <u>ISaBella</u>
She (or he) (or it!) looks like this

And then my other friends are

Summer Avalene Elsye Jake
Eilana Laotanae Elaenor
morgen Ashley Sofee
sarelete talore tegene
Olivea

We have a friend named Prairie!

My other friends look like this

My imaginary friends are named

OKeKa OMae MaBelle
PlaWese Stase

They look like this

I have friends that no one else can see, but they're not imaginary. One is named Ociceo, but I can't tell you the other's name. It's secret.

My best friend to have a secret with is
~~weird fairy~~ IsaBella or
Olivea

My best friend to make potions with is

Summer

My best friend to dig for
buried treasure with is

Bean! Duh!

Avelen and Elsy
Evelyn   Elsie

Amazing People

Who can hold her breath the longest?

Vanessa's little
brother Toby can
hold his breath for
76 seconds!

Who can do a backbend?

me

ZUZU!

Who can burp on purpose?

me and Elizabeth
(or Anna)

Dusit can burp the whole alphabet.

It's gross.

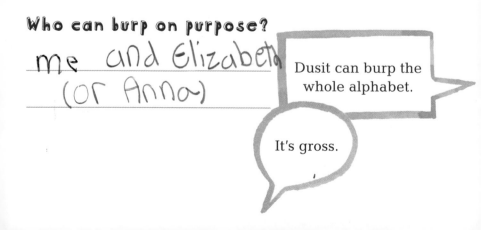

Who laughs the most?
m e

I am.

Who is the bravest?
m e

Yeah.
You are.

The wackiest thing
I ever did was

_____

_____

_____

_____

_____

_____

_____

_____

_____

_____

I would do it again.

☐ Yes   ☐ No

I live in

☑ a house   ☐ a cave

☐ an apartment   ☐ a castle

☐ a tent   ☐ a submarine

☐ a bus   ☐ a yurt

☐ a tree house

☐ something else that isn't on this list

Here's what it looks like

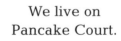

We live on
Pancake Court.

Here's what
it looks like.

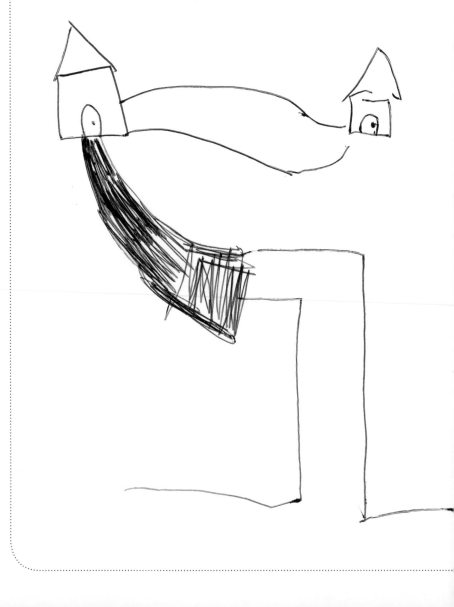

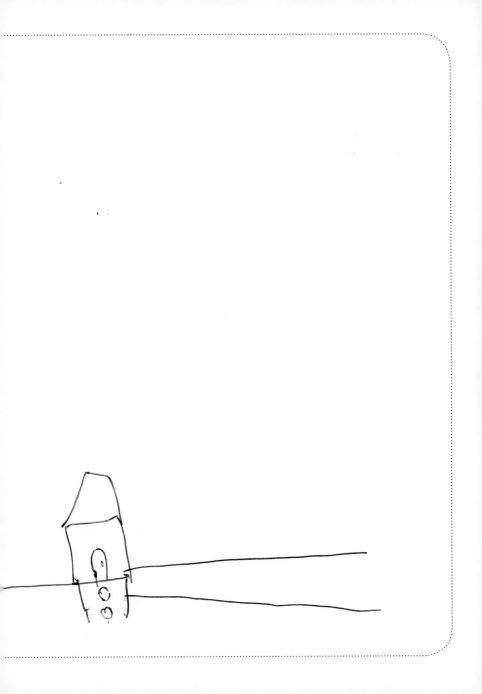

**If I could live anyplace,
I'd like to live in**

a Kingdom

I'd live in
a tree.

My favorite thing about my room is

thar lots of Spas

Ivy's room is amazing.
She's divided it up into
five little rooms.

Your room is nice, too.
It's so green.

**If I could have anything I wanted,
my room would look like this**

Dorr to Sekrit Art room

Scan to Enter

Sekrit siis dorr

Pooll that can Slid closd to be a floor

I would paint the walls this color

(Fill in the box with the color you want.)

My bed would be made out of

a ~~fluffu~~ fluffy clouD that never Falls

I'd sleep in
a giant shell hung
from the ceiling on silver
threads, so it would rock
back and forth.

I'd sleep in a hammock,
like pirates do.

There would be a secret password to get into my room and it would be

a invisaBel

Secret.

hanD Scaner

that only I

can See!

(Cover this up with a paper flap so no one can see it!)

I wouldn't have a password. I'd have a moat.

My favorite color is

(Fill in the box with the color.)

My favorite day of the week is

(Circle the day.)

Mon   Tue   Wed   Thu   Fri   Sat   Sun

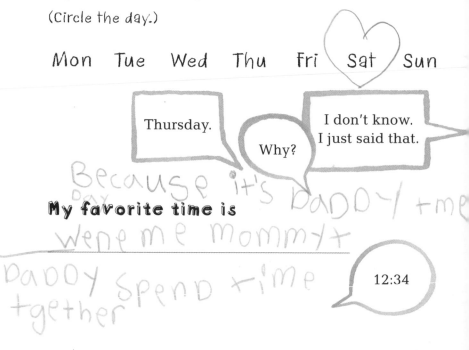

Thursday.

Why?

I don't know.
I just said that.

My favorite time is

Because it's Daddy time wene me mommy + Daddy spend time tgether

12:34

My favorite holiday is
Christmas and Esaetr

My favorite season is Summer

My favorite ice-cream flavor is

cholite cips and cokie
Doue Ice cream

My favorite kind of cake is

vnilae

I hope my next birthday cake
looks like this

Things I collect are

gems and ciristels and
shop cins

The thing I would most like to find is

a fariy, gold, more gems

A magic wand.

A dirt bike.

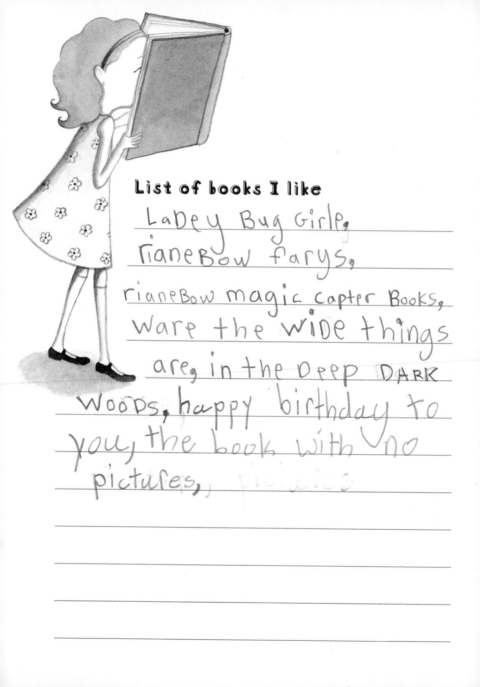

List of books I like

Labey Bug Girle,
rianeBow farys,
rianeBow magic capter Books,
ware the wide things
are, in the Deep DARK
Woods, happy birthday to
you, the book with no
pictures,

List of books I don't like

The animal I would most like to be is

a unacorne

The animal I would most like to have as a pet is

a unacorne a Butterfliy
a kittine and a fish that
all nere aver
Diye

I wish I had a tiny monkey.

What I really want is a sloth, but a kitten would be nice, too.

The animal I do have as a pet is

1 Dog 2 cats 1 fish

My pet's name is Roky cinoer Ella

It looks like this cage

Dog↓

cat↓

cat↓

Fish↓

List of good pet names

heather vilote sshapow
Lucky buttons Cherry
bells gemstons Fruit-cup
pearl Snow-fall
frosting-hearts Cutie
Star-light Springcles
loveday Candals heart-glow
Angel Cupcake frost
Christmas-tree Candy Cans
tosie-pop Popcorn dreams
fluffy
Ma-na-na
Opel oreo
Ella Cinder

Ugthorpe,
Bolivia,
Fruit Cup.

You are
so weird.

List of good kid names

Naomi Emma Anna
Alexa Olivia Molly
Isabella Eloises Kristy

I know a kid named Toad.

That's pretty good.

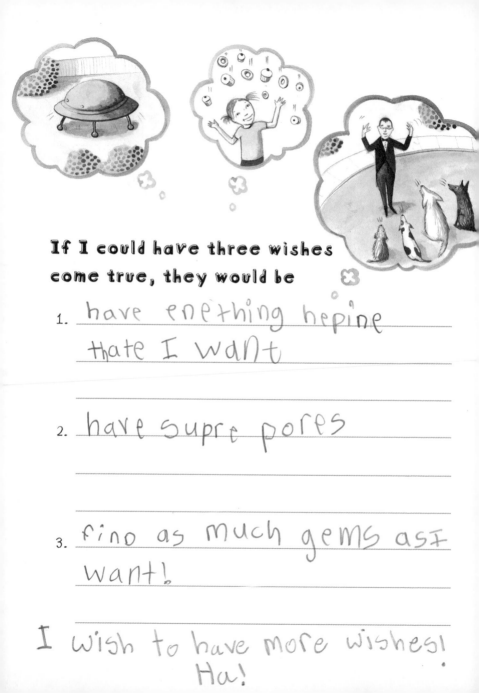

If I could have three wishes come true, they would be

1. have enething hepine thate I want

2. have supre pores

3. fino as much gems asI want!

I wish to have more wishes! Ha!

**If I had to pick one age
to be forever, I would be**

SEVEN

SEVEN!

**If I were going to get
one superpower, it would be**

to cpnchrolp the wether or
to DO enething that hast to
Do with gems

Flying, for sure.

What about
shape-shifting?
Then you could fly
if you wanted to.

You're right.
Shape-shifting.

Things that give me the creeps are

spiyoers Bees and Rats
3 Snacks

My worst enemy is _Bad Deams_
and all the trobel
because _I Just don't like it!..._
A LOT!

Mrs. Trantz.
She's so mean.

I'm not sure.
Mrs. Trantz is pretty
bad, but at least she
can't run very fast.

_p.s._
and
homwork

Would You Rather . . . ?

(Circle your choice.)

Eat an **ant** or a **feather**

ant

Lots of people eat ants.

Eat a **snail** or step in **dog poop**

Snail

Snail!

Dog poop!

Go **shopping** for ladies'
clothes for three hours
or
go to a **wedding** where
you were the only kid

WEDDING

Eat **lima beans** or
raw **cauliflower**

cauliflower

Would You Rather . . . ?

(Circle your choice.)

Break your **arm** or your **leg**

a r m

Be eaten by a **shark** or a **lion**

shark

Be able to **fly**
or **breathe underwater**

fly

Be a **fairy** or a **witch**

fairy

. . . **witch** or **mermaid**

mermaid

. . . **mermaid** or **unicorn**

unicorn ♡

. . . **unicorn** or **dragon**

unicorn

If I could make one magic potion that would really work, it would be

Fly

INVISIBILITY SPELL

INGREDIENTS

PREPARATIO

I want a potion to make me invisible. Then I can play tricks on people and they won't know who did it. And then I'll laugh really hard.

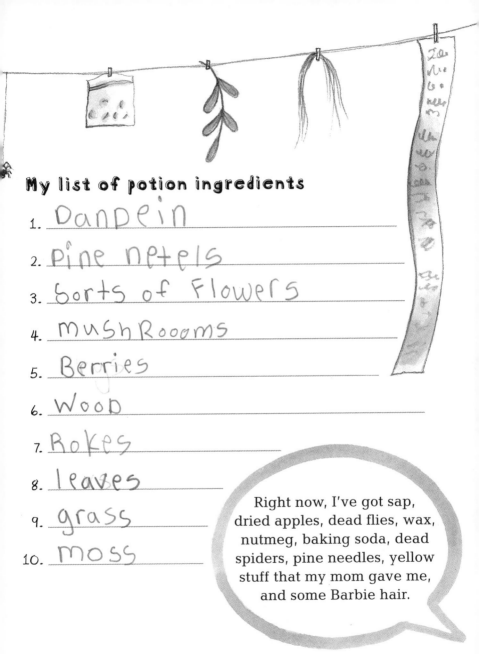

My list of potion ingredients

1. Danpein
2. Pine netels
3. Sorts of Flowers
4. mushRoooms
5. Berries
6. Wood
7. Rokes
8. leaves
9. grass
10. moss

Right now, I've got sap, dried apples, dead flies, wax, nutmeg, baking soda, dead spiders, pine needles, yellow stuff that my mom gave me, and some Barbie hair.

My favorite dinosaur is

troodon

Those Pachycephalosaurus guys were great! They had really thick skulls that they cracked together when they fought. They were not so smart, I bet.

I like Troodon. They had red eyes.

**The world record
I'd like to break is**

most gems

**The world record I might
really break is**

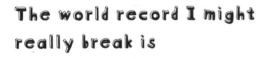

most gems

My favorite babysitter is

Both

because thar Both rilly nice

Leona, because she can draw perfect horses.

The thing that the babysitter lets me do that my parents don't is

thay let kitee come over

Leona lets me make my own snacks.

The latest I ever stayed up was

10:30

because of aunt silena

The nicest thing I ever did was

wene another persine sane
some girel was
mene I mane
fraens withe
her

The most trouble I ever got into was

Wean me and
IsaBell a Brok
all my trerse.
and wene me and
Kelly prue a map to have
a play bate in the mitele
of the nitge

A really bad word I would never say is

(Write it in the box and then erase it!)

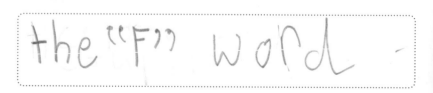

the "F" word

**When I get in trouble,
my grown-ups take away**

☐ Dessert

☐ TV

☐ My computer

☐ My favorite toys

☐ They don't take things away,
  but I have to stay in my room

☒ Other

All of the above.
Sheesh.

Something that was less fun than I expected was

Irning to cont By 2

Something that was more fun than I expected was

Irning to tell time

If I had to be in a ballet, I'd like
my costume to look like this

List of things I do to help stop climate change

rcielle Paper anD plstic

The most money I ever found on the sidewalk was

Quarter

If I had $10, I'd spend it on

gem minDing
Kit

A doll coffin.

If I had $20, I'd spend it on

10 piceis of golD

A leaf blower.

If I ran a camp, it would be called

Discovrey world 🌐

Camp Flaming Arrow!

Camp Neanderthal Flaming Arrow!

At my camp the rules would be

Do eneyting the Art
tEchrs say includin
they Discovrey
techrs say

At my camp the activities would be

Art, frstaid, Discovrey class, grat histrey, and Dansing, and minding for gems 3 glold

List of crafts I like

makeing frenoship
Braclits

List of crafts I think are dumb

I Dot thing any pocte are
BaD

Anything where you
have to be really careful.

Seven Falls.

My favorite movie is

DenDens

If I were a spy, my code name would be

vilote

My list of spying tips

Spiyin outsiDe
Spiyin insiDe
Spiyin from
winDow!

Three mysterious things that have happened to me are

1. Who made a nois in the School Bath room wene I wase alone?

2.

3.

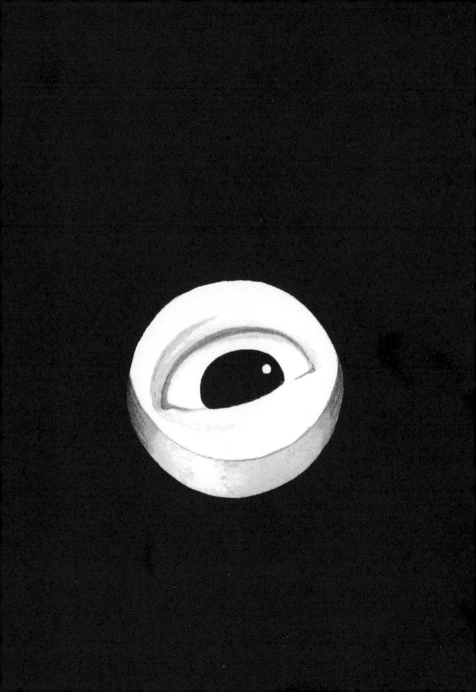

I have seen a ghost

☐ yes ☑ no

. . . and it looked like this

gosts are't real

There was a ghost
in the bathroom
at our school!

If I wanted to hide a diamond, I'd put it

in a secrit palse

There's a secret place that nobody knows about but me, and it's

(Cover this up with a paper flap so no one can see it!)

me and summer's hide out

A really great
April Fools' Trick is

Put on Fack
earings and say
you got them
perst, but you
ditintt

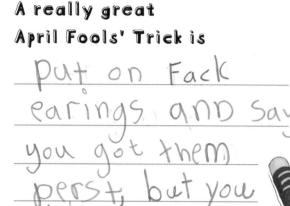

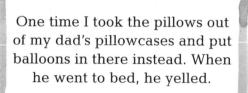

One time I took the pillows out
of my dad's pillowcases and put
balloons in there instead. When
he went to bed, he yelled.

**The last time I laughed really really
hard was when**

we we'r tukeing
aBote a Show

When my
dad yelled.

Something I did that was probably not a good idea

lafe to harD,
Play a prank,

Something I did that was a good idea

help clen the hous

Something I did that other people copycatted

My writing
and drawings
and Colerings

Presents I'd like to get that I might really get

more gems

**Presents I'd like to get that
I probably won't get**

golo ano silvre

A doll coffin.

Dirt!

**Presents I'd like to get that
I definitely won't get**

a unacorn (or fairy)

The last time I was really really surprised was when

mommy let me have a-Buch of gummy Baers

Design your own backpack

I am in ___frist___ grade,

Our teacher is
Ms. Aruba-Tate!

and my teacher is ___Mrs.Williams___

One time in school we

We wer' learning about soft "g" and my name has a soft g so I rised my hand and siad "Giulianna"

_____ **and everyone laughed.**

My favorite grown-up at school is

MRA. MCRAE

Ms. Aruba-Tate!

The scariest grown-up at school is

noun

Rose the
Yard Duty!

(No wone is)

My favorite letter of the alphabet is

(Write it in the box.)

G.

Why?

It just is.

My favorite subject in school is

Free Chois, Jesus, Centers, and lunch!

P.S. Mostly Science

My favorite PE activity is

music ♩♫

Komodo Hunt

I also like to play

Jale

The best field trip we ever went on was

the hay ride

Ways school could be better are

is they did let us have
atlest a littel candy!

Fun Things You Can Do
So You Won't Be Bored

Make-It-Yourself Mystery:

Move the stuff in your house around.
Switch the photos on the wall around; put
the books in different places; put the living
room cushions on
different chairs.
See how long it
takes your
family to notice.

Straightjacket:

In this game, you have to walk
in a straight line until you
actually bump into something;
then you can turn.
Try to walk home
from school or your
friend's house this way.

We do this all
the time!

Buried Treasure:

Bury something good, but not too good, in the yard. Then make a treasure map of the spot and tape it to the back of the toilet in your house for the kids who will live there in the future to find.

I buried some tweezers. I dug them up later, though.

Think Like a Carrot:

Spend five minutes trying to make yourself look like a particular vegetable. No costume or makeup required—just try to bend yourself into the shape of a veggie. Think hard about being that vegetable. Make your grown-up guess which vegetable you are.

Hot Lava

Pretend the floor of your house is hot lava and try to get across the house  without touching it. You can stick pillows and books to step on in difficult spots, but you get extra credit if you use fewer than ten. Don't walk on the tables or the counters (but skootch across them on your tush if you can). If you have something you can roll on, like for instance a big ball or a skateboard, that's really good.

Measure Stuff

If you have a tape measure (you know, one of those cloth or plastic things with inches and centimeters on it), you can measure anything. It's fun to measure yourself. Did you know that the size of someone's neck is usually twice the size of that person's wrist? And twice the size of the neck usually equals the size of the waist? Crazy, but true!

Do you know that before they're five, kids can't reach over the top of their heads to touch their ears?

That's nuts! Why not?

Their heads are too big, and their arms are too little.

Long Live the Queen!

Someday you may meet a Queen (or a King), and you have to know how to behave.

#1. You have to curtsy when you meet the Queen. To practice curtsying, put one foot in front of the other (doesn't matter which); grab a little hunk of your clothes in each hand, lift it a tiny bit; tilt the top of you toward the Queen; and dip your knees a little. Don't fall over.

#2. You cannot turn your back on the Queen, so you have to know how to leave a room by walking backward without smashing into anything, which is also not allowed. Practice a lot.

#3. You cannot sneeze in front of the Queen. One way to not sneeze is to press hard on either side of your face. The Queen won't mind that at all.

Write with Your Toes

Why? Because your toes are just sitting there, doing nothing. Stick a pencil in between them, and try to write your name.

Go ahead! Use your toes to write something here

Sneaky

Practice walking without making any noise. If you succeed, you will be able to sneak up on people!

You will be able to get really close to squirrels!

You will be able to get up in the middle of the night and see how the house looks!

Write Your Own
Ivy and Bean Story

Here are the beginnings of some Ivy and Bean stories.
Finish them yourself.

(Write a title here.)

1. Ivy and Bean and the coking contest

Ivy closed her book and sighed. "We don't know how to make anything," she said.

"What do you mean?" yelped Bean. "I can make potholders!"

"I mean we don't know how to make cheese. Or soup. Or anything. We'd never survive on the prairie."

"I know how to make cereal," said Bean.

"They don't have cereal on the prairie," Ivy said. "They have soup."

"Fine," said Bean. "Let's make soup."

thay told thar mother
to take them to the
Stor to gite sope evine
thoe thay new thar
spost to make it
tharselvs".

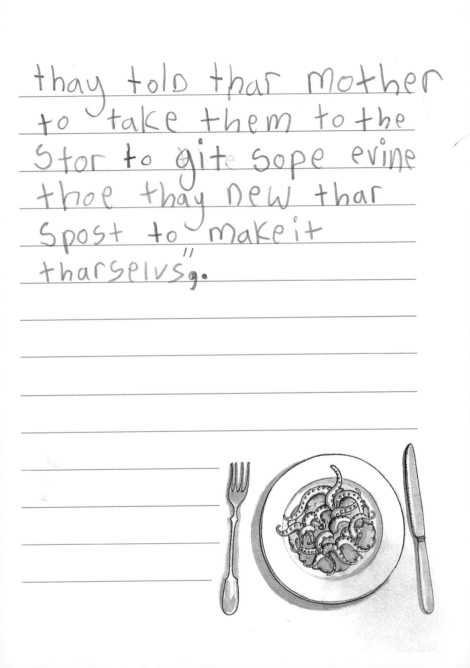

(Write a title here.)

2. _____

Bean's mom said she would buy Bean a
book. Any book Bean wanted. At the store,
Bean found a really cool sushi pencil-topper.
"A book," said Bean's mom. Bean found a
set of bug stickers. "A book!" said Bean's
mom. Bean found a kit for making your own
tattoos. "A BOOK!" said Bean's mom. So
Bean found a book called *Sing, Sing, Sing—
in Hawaiian!* What a great book!

_____

_____

_____

_____

_____

"You wanna play?" Bean hollered into Ivy's mail slot.

It took Ivy a moment to open the door, and when she did, she was wearing curtains.

Bean looked at her. "Why are you wearing that?"

"I think I'm becoming a mind-reader," Ivy whispered.

"You are?" Bean whispered back. "How do you know?"

"When the phone rang this morning, I knew it was Grandma," Ivy explained. "And it *was*." She smiled mysteriously.

"Okay, what am I thinking about right—now!" Bean yelled.

"Elephants," said Ivy.

And you know what? Bean *was* thinking about elephants! A long line of elephants, shaking their heads from side to side.

"Wow," Bean said. "That's amazing."

Ivy nodded. "I know. And it just came over me this morning." Suddenly, she froze. "Shh!" she whispered, looking toward the door. "There's someone out there, thinking. I can hear it!"

Are there any questions we forgot?

Write them down! Then answer them!

Q: _____

_____

A: _____

_____

Q: _____

_____

A: _____

_____

Q: _____

_____

A: _____

_____

_____

Q: _____

_____

A: _____

_____

Q: _____

_____

A: _____

_____

Q: _____

_____

A: _____

_____

_____

Any more thoughts?

Quick, write them down before you forget!

_____

_____

_____

_____

_____

_____

_____

_____

_____

_____

_____

_____

_____

YOU DID IT!

You wrote an entire book.

Practice your autograph here

_____

ISBN 978-1-4521-3729-2

Manufactured in China.

MIX
Paper from
responsible sources
FSC® C020056

Design by Kayla Ferriera.
Typeset in Blockhead and Candida.
The illustrations in this book were rendered in Chinese ink.

10 9 8 7 6 5

Chronicle Books LLC
680 Second Street
San Francisco, CA 94107

Chronicle Books—we see things differently.
Become part of our community at www.chroniclekids.com.

ANNIE BARROWS has written 87,614 words about Ivy and Bean. She is also the author of *The Magic Half* and its forthcoming sequel, *Magic in the Mix*. Her adult books include the bestselling *The Guernsey Literary and Potato Peel Pie Society*.

SOPHIE BLACKALL has drawn Ivy and Bean more than 700 times. She has illustrated 20 picture books and written a few, too, including one for adults called *Missed Connections: Love, Lost & Found*.

To host an event with the author or illustrator of this book, please contact publicity@chroniclebooks.com.

HAVE EVEN MORE FUN WITH IVY + BEAN!

Make your own buttons!

Create your own Ivy + Bean adventures with paper dolls!

More than 90 removable stickers!

Send secret notes to your friends!

Includes fold-and-seal notes and stickers!